# RELIGIONS OF HUMANITY

Chelsea House Publishers
1974 Sproul Road, Suite 400
Broomall, PA 19008

The Chelsea House world wide web address is
www.chelseahouse.com

First Printing

1 3 5 7 9 6 4 2

*Left: One name for Jesus Christ is 'The Good Shepherd.' Jesus was put on earth to serve as a type of shepherd, to lead other men away from the power and effects of sin. Part of an early Christian tile mosaic at the Aula Theodoriana at Aquileia, Italy.*

*Opposite: The Taos Indians of Taos, New Mexico, have rebuilt a church that was destroyed by the U.S. Army in the mid-nineteenth century. The present-day Taos church is based on older Indian traditions; likewise, in early Christianity, worship buildings were based on pre-existent local traditions.*

Library of Congress Cataloging-
in-Publication Data Applied For:
ISBN: 0-7910-6623-1

Design by Jaca Book

Original French text by
Julien Ries

00045783

# JULIEN RIES

## THE FIRST CENTURIES OF

# CHRISTIANITY

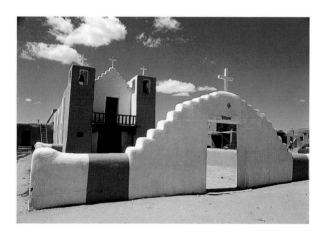

CHELSEA HOUSE PUBLISHERS
PHILADELPHIA

*Jesus followed the practice of the times by washing the feet of his followers before the Last Supper. Jesus, the master, also became the companion of the followers, or Apostles, in all ways. Armenian miniature from an ancient text, the Vaspurkan Codex.*

# CONTENTS

# INTRODUCTION

This small volume will provide a quick overview of the first four centuries of our era when the Church founded by Christ established its firm roots in the ancient world. The limits of this period are provided by two books: the first is the *Acts of the Apostles* which records the events of the first thirty years of Christian life and evangelization, while the second is marked by *The City of God* written by St. Augustine between 412 and 426 A.D., a masterpiece which covers the vast extent of history.

Born among the people of Israel from whom it inherited the ideas of the promise and of prophets, Christianity soon went its own separate way since the paschal community retained a very vivid experience of the mission imparted by the risen Christ and confirmed by the Holy Spirit on Pentecost Day. Under the leadership of the apostles, the Gospel spread rapidly until, at the beginning of the second century, the Greco-Roman world started to react. Some Christian writers, called Apologists from a Greek word meaning 'to defend,' strongly criticized the idols and their cults although they insisted on the Christians' civic allegiances. In spite of persecutions, Christian values managed to penetrate society: the new culture of the new faith spread in a society prepared by Hellenism, which encompasses fundamental Greek cultural elements in the ancient world. The third century saw the affirmation of the Christian way of life. Five chapters of this book will show the progress of the Church during the first two centuries.

The Roman Empire had a religious foundation that became accentuated in the third century by the emperor being viewed as a god. The emperors tried to react against internal crises and external threats in various ways, including the relaunching of the sacred: the cult of the emperor and the cults of the protecting gods. The Christians became the victims of the new ideology and of the persecutions that arose from it. In 313 Constantine confirmed at Milan an edict which allowed religious liberty. The Church continued to organize itself and to react against Gnosticism and Manichaeism, forms of religious-philosophical thinking that threatened to introduce errors among the Christian community. Moreover, it had clarified the rules of faith to its opponents. By the time it learned to find its freedom, there was already a Christian fabric in the weave of society. The last five chapters of this book will describe the events of these two centuries.

It was not deemed relevant to start this brief account with a biography of Jesus Christ. This was done to stress the fact that the first Christian communities did not consider themselves as followers of the dead master but rather, they felt invigorated by the presence of the Son of God who had risen from the dead and was, therefore, still alive. The life of the Christian communities should therefore be considered—from their own point of view—as the life of Jesus Christ himself, just as he had promised the disciples at his ascension into Heaven following the Resurrection: 'Behold, I am with you at all times, even to the end of the world' (Mt., 28, 20).

*In East Harlem, New York City in the early 1960s, a number of Protestant parishes used space in old shops and stores to reach out to and serve Puerto Ricans and other immigrants. Their lives were made difficult by the effects of poverty, drugs, and violence.*

# 1
# FROM APOSTOLIC PASCHAL COMMUNITY TO THE FIRST CHRISTIAN COMMUNITIES

Following the events of Easter Sunday which took place towards 30 A.D., the apostles, together with some of the disciples of Jesus who had been frightened and scattered by the events that had unfolded on Golgotha, started once again living a communitarian form of life they had lived with their master. In the *Acts of the Apostles* Luke describes this specific context and the activities of this enthusiastic group conscious of the presence of the Risen Christ among them during meetings, meals, and projects. An unprecedented event predicted by Jesus took place: the gift of the Holy Spirit, the creation of the Church as an event in sacred history (*Acts*, 2, 1-4). After Pentecost the apos-

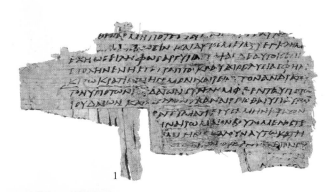

1

2

tles and the disciples formed a community assiduous in prayer, conscious of having received a permanent injunction to evangelize the world, and characterized by the remembrance of the signs and words of Jesus. They formed a community identifiable by the behavior of its members who diligently followed the teachings of the apostles, by its fraternal unity, and by the breaking of the bread within their houses, just as Jesus had asked them to do in remembrance of the Last Supper that had taken place before his crucifixion.

A new people was in the making (*Acts*, 15, 14-18). The rapid succession of conversions brought about the opposition of the Jewish authorities, followed by the persecution and dispersal of the Jerusalem community. New communities were formed in the synagogues and even among pagans. Some collections of the words of Jesus, soon integrated in the *Gospels*, which were still in the process of definitive formation, constituted a sort of memorandum of the oral tradition of those who had personally witnessed and intensely lived the faith. In Galilee and in Syria, Greek-speaking Hellenistic communities lived side by side

with Aramaic-speaking Judaeo-Christin communities. Struck on the road to Damascus, Saul of Tarsus converted from being the persecutor of the new religion to its apostle. The word *Ekklesia* came to refer to the real Israel: it was a religious and cultural concept at a time which gave expression to the free choice of God and the unity among the believers within communities characterized by great social and ethnic diversities.

The rapid spread of the new religion in Palestine and in Syria, together with the numerous Judaeo-Christian and Hellenistic communities existing side by side, caused tensions to spring up and grow. The Judaeo-Christians wanted to impose circumcision and other Jewish Mosaic practices on new converts from paganism. In 49 A.D. the incident at Antioch and the Council of Jerusalem brought the matter to an end (*Acts*, 15, 2-10; *Gal.* 2, 11). The authority of the apostles and the firmness of Peter and Paul saved the unity of the newly born Church, which they would confirm with their martyrdom in Rome under Nero. The fall of Jerusalem in 70 A.D. served to sever definitely Christianity from the government of Israel.

**1.** *The library Biblioteca Laurenziana, in Florence, Italy, holds a scroll with the oldest existing part of the* Acts of the Apostles. *It is probably from the late second century.*
**2.** *In the 1970s after the Second Vatican Council, the ceremony of the Eucharist could once again be celebrated in a home, rather than only in a church. This renewed a tradition that dates back to the early days of Christianity.*

3

**3.** *An Egyptian ancient book with a miniature of the Pentecost is stored in Paris, France. The Holy Spirit descends on the Apostles gathered around Mary.*
**4.** *In the third century at Dura Europos in Syria, there were several different religions, even Jewish and Christian communities. This fresco shows the Temple of Solomon, the most sacred place for the Jews. For the first Christians, the Eucharist could be celebrated in any building.*

4

**5.** *An early Christian flat sculpture, or bas relief, shows Peter and Paul embracing each other. This demonstrates the unity between the two 'founders' of Christianity. They had a common goal despite having different homelands and cultures. This sculpture is in the Paleo-Christian Museum at Aquileia, Italy.*

5

# THE RAPID SPREAD OF CHRIST'S MESSAGE

Shortly after its foundation, Christianity reached Antioch in Syria and Damascus where a community of Hellenized Christians established itself. 'At Antioch the disciples were called Christians for the first time' (*Acts*, 11, 26). It is from Antioch as well that, in 45 A.D., a mission left for Asia Minor which was to mark the start of the ministry of Paul, who was accompanied by Barnabas. They first turned to the Jewish communities, then to the proselytes and the pagans. Paul's strategy can be clearly seen in Chapter 13 of the *Acts*. It also shows how, following the opposition and the refusal of the Jews, he slowly elaborated his own theology of conversion for the pagans.

In the forties, Jewish nationalism started to lose its patience and began exerting an ever-stronger pressure on Christian Jews. Thanks to Paul's efforts, the Christian message rapidly made its way into the pagan world. Following the decisions taken at Jerusalem in 49 A.D., Pauline Christianity dissociated itself completely from the temporal destiny of Israel. In 50 A.D. Paul undertook a new missionary journey. Following stops in Asia Minor, he turned to Europe (Macedon, Achaia). After passing through Athens, in 51-52 he stopped at Corinth and then returned to Antioch by way of Ephesus and Jerusalem. Silas, Timothy, and Luke accompanied him in the foundation of these Churches.

In the spring of 53, Paul left on another journey, passing through Galatia and Phrygia, before settling down for three years at Ephesus (54-57) to preach the Gospel in the synagogues and to the pagans. Returning through Greece, he visited Macedon, Corinth with Titus, Tyre, and Miletus before arriving in Jerusalem in 58 A.D. in time for Pentecost. The Judaeo-Christian opposition to him had kept growing since 49 A.D. and the nationalists arrested him. Eventually, after a number of adventures, he was martyred in Rome under Nero.

Towards 112 A.D. Pliny the Younger, the governor of Bithynia in Asia Minor, wrote to Emperor Trajan about the Christians. Following inquiries he had found that they were responsible for the decline of pagan sacrifices in the cities and in the country. Pliny confirms what is already known from the Apostolic Fathers: the extraordinary rapid spread of Christianity starting from the end of the first century, the organization of the community, the celebration of the Eucharist on the Lord's Day, the shaping of Christian symbols and rituals, and the unity of the group living in a pagan world subject to Rome.

2

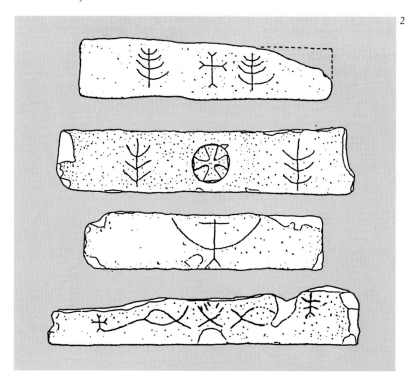

3

Christian presence in the first century.

Christian presence in the second century.

Christian presence in the first and second centuries.

1

**1.** A very old fresco from the catacombs of Saint Callixtus in Rome shows a fish and some small loaves of bread. This refers to the miracle of the fish and the bread. Also, 'fish' was the anacronym of 'Jesus Christ Son of God the Savior' in Greek. The bread is symbol of his body in the ceremony of the Eucharist.

4

First journey of St. Paul
Second journey
Third journey
Journey to Rome

**2.** Drawings from houses in the early days of Christianity showing both Jewish (the seven-branched candelabrum) and Christian (the cross and the fish) symbols.

**3.** The map shows the first Christian communities at the time of the apostles and the journeys of Paul to form and encourage these communities.

**4.** In 112 A.D., Pliny the Younger was the Roman governor in Bithynia on the Black Sea. Pliny was surprised by the unity of the Christians and wrote to Emperor Trajan about his concerns.

# 3
# THE CONFLICT BETWEEN PAGANS AND CHRISTIANS

In the second century the extraordinary vitality of Christianity started to attract attention and to foster uneasiness since it was an odd religion, which refused to worship false gods or false cults. This monotheism, the cult of a one and only God, was looked upon as a dangerous form of atheism, similar to not having any god at all. Various rumors of strange Christian practices fed popular suspicion: the adoration of a donkey's head, the sacrifice of children, incest, and orgies. In 177 A.D. Celsus wrote *Logos Alethes*, a 'discourse of truth,' which contemptuously referred to Christianity's origins, Jesus the founder, and the doctrine itself as being unworthy of a reli-

gion. He contrasted the 'mystic madness of the Christians' with the values of other religions, Hellenic culture, and the wisdom of the barbarians. Born in 233, the Neo-Platonic philosopher Porphyry wrote a *Treatise on Divine Images* and a *Treatise Against the Christians*, the latter mostly lost, in which he attacked the Christian scriptures, denied the resurrection of Jesus, confuted the sacraments, and reproached the Christians for their disrespect to the statues of the gods. In the name of Hellenic culture, he asked for help against Christianity.

The Christian Apologists picked up the challenge. Justin, a Greek philosopher who was martyred in Rome in 165 A.D., wrote two *Apologies* in which he refuted the accusations and attacked the idols, which he described as mere statues made by men and raised in temples as gods. He contrasted Jesus and the realization of the prophecies with the pagan gods, although he also found some common features in the two, the sign that 'the seed of the Word is innate in all mankind' (*Apol.*, II, 8, 1). Tertullian (155-225), who was born in Africa and had a refined Latin culture, wrote his *Ad Nationes* (To the Nations) and *Apologeticum* (Speech for the Defense). An expert in law, he refuted all the accusations against the Christians, asked for freedom of worship on their behalf, and then attacked the pagan gods, who could not feel either disrespect or homage. Like a good lawyer, he demolished the cult of the emperor, stressing the devotion of the Christians who were to be found all over the empire and who constituted its force: 'We have

The third approach is taken from demonology, which means the study of demons and which was extremely popular at that time. Various apologists showed how devils hide beneath the appearance of the statues of pagan gods. Augustine made use of these ideas in his *De civitate Dei* (The City of God).

The popularity of the image of the Good Shepherd in early Christian art was the answer to the accusations of lack of piety and madness, since it represented the careful solicitude of the God of the Christians.

3

just been born and we have already filled the earth and all that belongs to you' (*Apologet.*, 37, 4). A contemporary of Tertullian, Minucius Felix also wrote a Christian apology in the form of a dialogue entitled *Octavius*. It listed both the attacks against the Christians and firm replies based on proving the pagan gods were false ones.

Christian apologists made use of three approaches. The first is that of Philo of Alexandria, a first-century philosopher who made use of the deification of the elements, the stars, idolatry, zoolatry, and pagan mythology to highlight their baseness. It was the approach favored by Latin Apologists.

The second approach was drawn from the 'ideas of the Greek writer Evemerus (c. 340-c.260 B.C.), according to whom the gods were only deified illustrious individuals. This approach was used against the cult of the emperor.

*1. A thoughtful goddess Athena in a fifth-century B.C. Greek statue. The statue represents the doubts attacking first Greek society and then Graeco-Roman society about the spiritual future of man.*
*2. Christ is shown as a donkey in a second-to-third-century drawing. This drawing ridicules the Christian belief that a god could become man and allow himself to be killed.*
*3. One of the oldest frescoes of Christ as 'The Good Shepherd' in the catacombs of Saint Callixtus in Rome. He is not a ridiculous god-donkey, but a god-made-into-man to accompany and look after mankind, just like a shepherd looks after his flock.*

# 4
# THE INCULTURIZATION OF CHRISTIANITY IN THE HELLENISTIC WORLD

1

**1.** *The Christians saw the value of Greek culture and its philosophers quite early. This tile mosaic from Syria of the first centuries A.D. shows the philosopher Socrates with other wise men.*

At the end of the second century Alexandria became the crucible where the Gospels came across Greek culture. In Alexandria, Clement, a convert to Christianity and a great traveler, joined the *didaskaleion*, a Christian center of higher studies run by Pantaenus the philosopher, whom he would actually succeed towards 200. Making use of his excellent knowledge of Philo, Clement elaborated a vast project of catechesis that brought together the teachings of the Gospels, Greek philosophy, and some basic elements of Hellenism. His *Exhortation to the Greeks*, the *Protrepticus*, was a proposal to idolaters to convert, but which presented the 'new song' (instead of the fine melodies of Orpheus, the supreme singer in Greek mythology) instead of the pagan mysteries, the most widespread religious experiences of the time. Clement then analyzed the various philosophers, showing how they all provided evidence of divine transcendence. A philosopher and a humanist, he placed philosophy at the service of the knowledge of the Scriptures so as to lead to a scientific knowledge and to change mere opinion into certainty, which he calls the true *gnosis* (knowledge). Truth is the illumination of man and the world by means of the divine *Logos* (the Word) which came to renew the entire cosmos (*Protr.* IX-XII). In using the vocabulary of *soteria* (sal-

vation), so fundamental to Hellenistic thought, he developed the entire perspective of salvation through Christ. The *Stromateis* (Tapestries) analyze the relationship between the new religion and profane science as a preparation for the gospel: philosophy, the gift of God to the Greeks; symbolism which provides an access to the divine mysteries; and initiation that is the introduction to penetrating the heart of the mystery itself.

Inspired by Christ, the Logos, the Christian lives in the image of God. Clement made Alexandria the center of Christian culture. Inherited from the primitive Christian Church, the practices that still bear a Jewish imprint take on a Hellenistic garb. The heritage of rhetoric and of ancient philosophy were also assimilated thanks to Clement and his successors. As a reaction to certain Encratite tendencies in Palestine, which stressed the evil in matter, a form of Christianity emerged which conformed to the Hellenistic ideal of man. According to Jean Daniélou, 'a process of sociological uprooting from Judaism' took place in Alexandria. Significantly, Christian iconography included Orpheus among the symbols that pre-announced Christ and his new song.

**2.** *Philosophers speak with each other on a third-to-fourth-century Christian sarcophagus. The Christians adopted different parts of Greek knowledge that agreed with their new faith.*
**3.** *As a result of the spread of Christianity, old Roman public assembly houses were changed into churches. These ruins are in Djemila, Algeria.*

# 5
# CHRISTIAN SOCIETY IN THE THIRD CENTURY

Among the documents most useful for understanding the developments in Christian society in the third century, pride of place must be given to the works of Clement of Alexandria, Origen, Tertullian, and Hippolytus of Rome.

Initiation to Christianity was through a cathecumenate, which was organized systematically by the hierarchy and firmly installed by the end of the second century. A candidate had to pass an admission test, attend regular meetings for religious instruction, and receive a positive assessment of one's preparation. Administration of baptism was by means of a triple immersion in water followed by subsidiary rites and by receiving the Eucharist in the presence of the bishop. Baptism of children was already practiced. Together with public and private penance, there were also rites of reconciliation, an authentic sacrament that included the confession of sins to a priest. During the third century the remission of sins became the subject of a controversy between strict and more permissive authorities.

The organization of the hierarchy was uniformly fixed: the episcopate, the presbyterate, and the deaconate, three orders that were conferred by the laying of hands by the bishop, a tradition that firmly respected the primitive apostolic tradition. A number of ministries were conferred by bishops but did not need ordination: widows who looked after sick people and deaconesses and virgins dedicated to teaching and supporting neophytes.

The Christian communities included various assemblies, the most important being the Eucharist on the 'day of the Lord' preceded by prayer and concluded by the giving of the kiss of peace, a tradition that dated back to the earliest days. There were daily assemblies of the faithful with the priests and deacons for the purpose of praying and teaching, from which numerous homilies have survived. There was also the evening assembly, which took place at the time when the lamps were lit, sometimes followed by an agape, which is a community meal. The ruins of the church of Dura Europos (256) and some frescoes show the first diffusion of Christian art connected with meeting places and sacred buildings.

Continuously growing in number, the Christians lived within society, sharing the same language, the same food, and the same dress. However, a style of Christian life also developed. Clement and Tertullian indicated the differences from a pagan way of life: a simple life without excessive luxury, food and wine in moderation without drunkenness or orgies, baths, shows, and sport but not pagan or immoral games. The family represented a cherished value: divorce and abortion were

condemned, the education of children was greatly encouraged, and one was expected to stay away from all that was idolatrous. As far as civic duties were concerned, there was great reserve concerning the official cult, while military service was carefully evaluated with discrimination. Death represented the important moment not only for martyrs but also for every Christian. Of this the catacombs and the cemeteries bear eloquent testimony.

*1. This present-day Christian community in a Latin American village resembles the earliest communities.*
*2. Clement was one of the leaders of the Church in the second and third centuries. Here is the school of Alexandria where Clement taught students from various countries.*
*3. A fresco in the catacombs in Via Latina in Rome. It shows Samson beating the Philistines. It also prefigures Christ expelling the merchants from the temple.*

# THE CULT OF THE EMPEROR AND THE PERSECUTION OF THE CHRISTIANS

**1.** *This group of statues shows the Tetrarchs who ruled the Western and the Eastern Roman Empires. It was transported from Constantinople to Venice. A new idea is already present in the culture of Rome. That idea is the need for agreement, even among rulers.*
**2.** *The back side of a Roman coin shows a head with the rays of the sun. The ancient cults of the sun had worshipped*

*a powerful star. The new cults worshipped the emperor and his political and military powers. Notice the shield on the coin.*
**3.** *A fresco from the catacombs of Commodilla in Rome shows Jesus between alpha and omega. These were the first and last letters of the Greek alphabet. The painting is saying that Jesus gives meaning to every thing in life, from the first to the last.*

1

2

The Roman Empire had a religious base that became even more pronounced in the third century when imperial power was given a sacred dimension. As a result of the great crisis brought about by the threats of the Persians, the German tribes, and civil wars, the emperors attempted to rectify matters with an energetic political transformation in a new religious climate: a profound sense of the sacrality of the world and of life; a sense of the divine expressed by the protecting gods of Rome; the sacred character of the emperor as a reflection of Jupiter; and a solar theology which made the emperor the son of *sol invictus*—'the invincible sun.' The cult of Mithras, a solar god of eastern origin, contributed to this development. Christianity became incompatible with this cult of the emperor and of Rome.

Already in 249 Emperor Decius had issued an edict ordering all citizens to show their devotion publicly to the protecting deities of Rome, by means of incense and of sacrifice. These two acts of worship were meant to re-create political and religious unity throughout the empire. Most Christians refused to obey and many were tortured and condemned to death. Supported by pagan public opinion, in 257 an edict issued by Valerian and Gallienus enjoined the bishops, the priests, and the deacons to sacrifice their gods. If they refused, they were to be punished with exile or death and the confiscation of all the wealth of the community in favor of the public treasury. The results of these persecutions are well known: there were many martyrs, but also many apostates—deniers of their faith—and there was a great fear for Christian unity for a time.

In 239 the tetrarchy was set up: the provinces of the empire were divided among Diocletian, Galerius, Maximian, and Constantius Chlorus. Motivated by the solar cult, a new sacralization of power opened the way for persecution, first of the Manichaeans, the followers of a religion of Persian origin (see Chapter 7) and then of the Christians (303). Churches were razed to the ground and bishops and leaders of the communities, especially in the East, in the regions of the Danube, and later in Africa were arrested and put on trial. Many people chose martyrdom, but many others preferred to apostatize. In the West a sort of calm followed the abdication of Diocletian, but in the East Galerius and Maximinus Daia started the persecutions afresh.

In 311, Galerius issued an edict of toleration that gave freedom for Christians to practice their cult, permission to rebuild their meeting places, and also requested them to pray for the safety of the emperor and the empire. In the East Maximinus renewed the persecution. However, Constantine, who obtained an important victory on October 28, 312, on February 313 confirmed in Milan Galerius' edict of toleration. On June 13, 313 it was published in Nicomedia for the entire East, thereby extending religious freedom to all Christians in the empire.

**4.** Part of a tile mosaic pavement in the church at Huarte in Syria. It shows fragments, or relics, being moved. The relics of the apostles and the first saints were highly prized in the churches built in their honor.

# CHRISTIAN THOUGHT FACING GNOSTICS AND MANICHAEANS

From the second century onwards, as Christianity spread in the countries of the Mediterranean, it started facing the opposition of the Gnostics. Gnosticism stressed the revelation of mystical knowledge to a select group who would thus obtain insight into the mysteries of the heavens, God, man, and the way to obtain salvation. According to such a dualist gnosis, that is one that includes the two original principles of the world, man is a stranger lost in a wicked world. A divine spark imprisoned by the matter of the body, his soul has to be re-awakened through initiation to find its path to salvation.

It was Irenaeus of Lyon who first realized the peril of such teaching. In his voluminous *Treatise against Heresies* (c. 180) he denounced the gnosis of the false name, confuted its errors, and contrasted it with the essential facts of Christianity: belief in the New Testament which has been most faithfully conserved; the value of traditions which derived from the

Apostles and apostolic witnesses; the dogma—a Greek word meaning 'doctrine' and which designates a truth of faith—of a unique God who was responsible for creation by means of the Word; the announcement of the Incarnation through the words of the prophets; the story of salvation; Christology—that is the mystery of Jesus Christ as understood by the Church—; the theology of creation, of the Incarnation, and of Redemption, that is reflections on the manifestations of the one God; Christian anthropology; and the search for the real aspect of man who was created in God's image and saved through Jesus.

Like Irenaeus, Tertullian attacked the Gnostic followers of Valentine who had preached his doctrine in Egypt and in Rome, but he also wrote a *Treatise against Marcion*, a Greek author and theologian who founded an ecclesial community in Rome in 144. He explained the rule of faith, refuted Gnos-

*1. 2. A rare portrait of Mani (left) from a Chinese painting. Mani's philosophy opposed the Christian concept of the Trinity. The Trinity is shown here in an early-Christian sculpture which also shows the creation of Eve as Adam lies sleeping.*

*The central sitting figure is God the Father. The son, Jesus Christ, is laying his hands on Eve's head. The Holy Spirit is represented by the person standing behind God the Father, following what is happening.*

tic terminology, and created a Latin theological vocabulary. A disciple of Irenaeus, Hippolytus of Rome wrote a *Confutation of all the Heresies*, which by means of a comparative study between pagan thought and about thirty Gnostic doctrines, attempted to show that Gnosis was a new form of Hellenistic paganism.

Born in 216, Mani spent his youth in the Judaeo-Christian sect of the Elkesaites of Dastumisan in Babylon. He reevaluated the Gnostic texts, and restructured them around the Light-Darkness myth and then founded a Gnostic Church on the model of the Christian Church. He presented himself as the personification of the Paraclete—the Spirit—foretold by Je-

sus and chose twelve apostles and seventy-two disciples. He then compiled his own Scriptures in which he attempted to integrate Christian doctrines with Buddhist and Zoroastrian ones. A religion of the book and a universal religion of salvation, Manichaeism presents itself as the real religion preached by Jesus and revealed to Mani by the Paraclete. The Fathers of the Church (see Chapter 9) organized a systematic rebuttal against the propaganda of the sect whose missionary zeal had extended to all parts of the empire and beyond. After a struggle that lasted a couple of centuries, St. Augustine, who had belonged to the sect for ten years, carried out the last great assault.

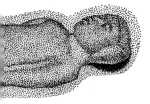

*3. The most basic idea of Christianity is the mercy of God. Christ spoke of this idea to the Samaritan woman who had come to draw water from the well. Christ told her that he was the salvation of man. The scene is from a fresco from the catacombs in Via Latina in Rome.*

# THE DEVELOPMENT OF CHRISTIANITY IN SOCIETY IN THE FOURTH CENTURY

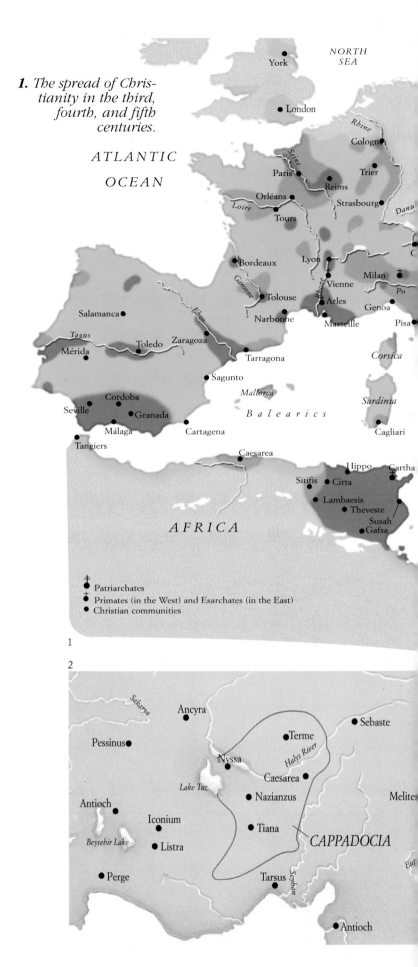

**1.** *The spread of Christianity in the third, fourth, and fifth centuries.*

By the beginning of the fourth century, the Church had already grown powerful within the Roman Empire. Bishops assisted by priests and deacons led the communities while widows and consecrated virgins were given a special status. Conversions in the countryside meant the creation of parishes where the bishops sent priests to look after the faithful. Conversions also took place beyond the limits of the empire: Persia, Armenia, the Caucasus, Ethiopia, and among the Goths near the Black Sea.

Religious life was centered on the celebration of the Eucharist, which was celebrated solemnly on Sundays and also during the week. The liturgical calendar became defined: celebrations in winter revolving around the mystery of the Incarnation and others in Easter centered on the Resurrection. Different liturgies also took root in the East and in the West, each with its own characteristics influenced by the culture of the people. The Churches legislated on their respective cults and on the administration of the sacraments. Thus adults were baptized on Easter Saturday. The sacrament of penance remains of great relevance as a result of the public reconciliation of penitents. In 325 Sunday was declared a feast day.

The cult of the martyrs, already in practice in the second century, spread even further as a result of the great persecutions: the belief in the intercession of saints in Heaven; the expectation of the manifestation of their miraculous powers; the belief in the resurrection of the body; and the veneration of relics. The celebration of the Eucharist took the place of the pagan funeral banquet (*refrigerium*) on the tomb of the deceased. The cult of relics came to assume great importance and the Church published directives to keep the devotion to saints within bounds.

Religious journeys known as pilgrimages became popular in the fourth century. Crowds used to make their way to the tombs and the sanctuaries of famous martyrs. They also visited holy sites known as *martyria* that were connected with the passion of Christ. These included Calvary, the Mount of Olives, and Bethlehem. Pilgrimage routes to Jerusalem were already established by 333.

Thanks to the influence of the pope and the bishops, the Church attempted to bend its law and customs towards a greater justice and charity. Prisons were more closely monitored, slaves were liberated, treatment of prisoners was checked, infanticide was prohibited, charitable institutions were developed, and hospitals and nursing groups were founded, as well as an increase in the giving of alms.

Anthony, the father of monasticism, died a centenarian in the Egyptian desert in 356. His disciples had built their own quarters near his cell, thus becoming the first anchorites or

hermits. In 323 Pachomius had gathered around him a number of monks at Tabennisi in Upper Egypt and gave them a rule of common life: this marked the origin of coenobitism. The various forms of monasticism made their way to Syria, Asia Minor, Italy, and Gaul.

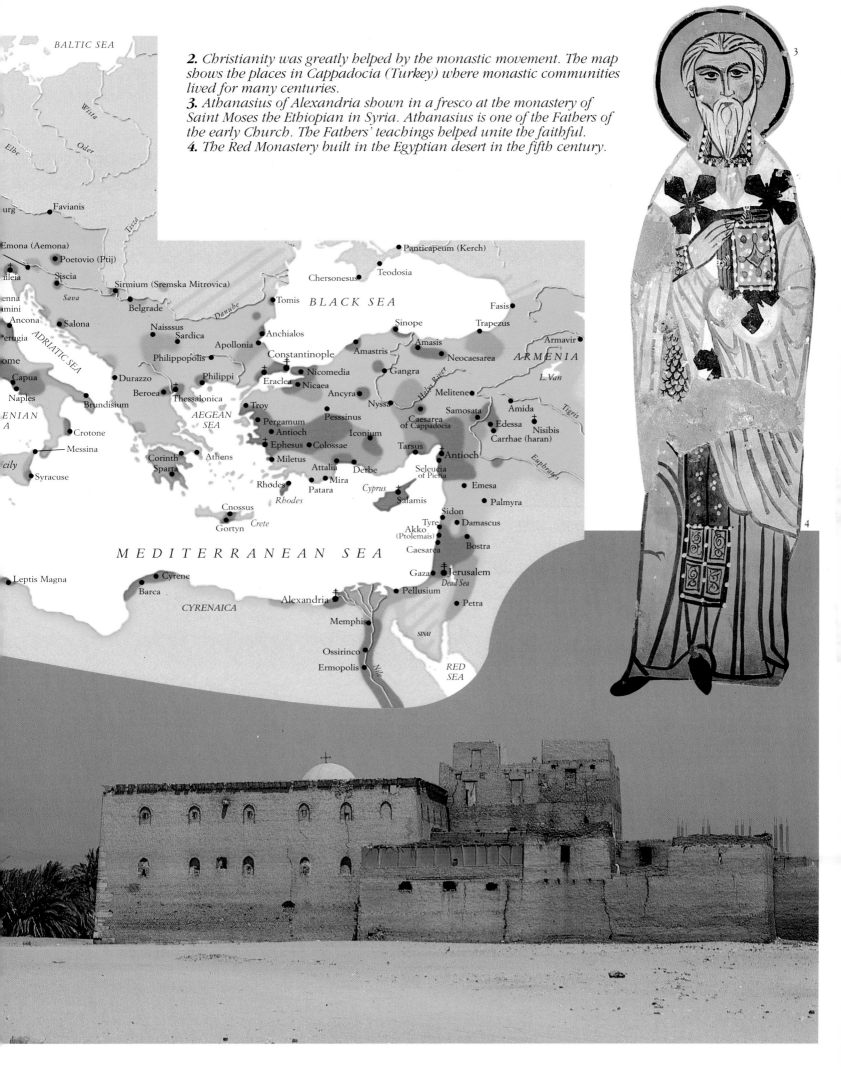

**2.** Christianity was greatly helped by the monastic movement. The map shows the places in Cappadocia (Turkey) where monastic communities lived for many centuries.
**3.** Athanasius of Alexandria shown in a fresco at the monastery of Saint Moses the Ethiopian in Syria. Athanasius is one of the Fathers of the early Church. The Fathers' teachings helped unite the faithful.
**4.** The Red Monastery built in the Egyptian desert in the fifth century.

BALTIC SEA

*Wisła*

*Elbe*

*Oder*

*Tisza*

*Sava*

Emona (Aemona)
Poetovio (Ptij)
Siscia
urg Favianis
Sirmium (Sremska Mitrovica)
Belgrade
Salona
Naisssus
Sardica
Philippopolis
Durazzo
Beroea
Thessalonica
Troy
Pergamum
Antioch
Ephesus Colossae
Miletus
Corinth
Sparta Athens
Rhodes
Patara Mira
Attalia Derbe
Cnossus
Gortyn *Crete*
*Rhodes*

*ADRIATIC SEA*

enna
mini
Ancona
erugia
ome
Capua
Naples
Brundisium
Crotone
Messina
Syracuse
cily
Leptis Magna
Barca
Cyrene
CYRENAICA
Alexandria
Memphis
Ossirinco
Ermopolis

Panticapeum (Kerch)
Chersonesus
Teodosia
Tomis
*BLACK SEA*
Sinope
Fasis
Trapezus
Anchialos
Apollonia
Constantinople
Amastris
Amasis
Neocaesarea
Nicomedia
Nicaea
Eraclea
Gangra
Ancyra
Nyssa
Pessinus
Iconium
Caesarea
of Cappadocia
Tarsus
Antioch
Seleucia
of Pieria
*Cyprus*
Salamis
Emesa
Palmyra
Sidon
Tyre Damascus
Akko
(Ptolemais) Bostra
Caesarea
Gaza Jerusalem
*Dead Sea*
Pellusium
Petra
*SINAI*
*RED SEA*
Melitene
Samosata
Amida
Edessa Nisibis
Carrhae (haran)
Armavir
*ARMENIA*
*L. Van*
*Tigris*
*Euphrates*

*AEGEAN SEA*

*MEDITERRANEAN SEA*

*Danube*

*Helys River*

*Nile*

ENIAN
A

Philippi

3

4

# CONSTANTINE AND THE CONVERSION OF THE EMPIRE

A Christian emperor, Constantine felt the responsibility to save Rome but he also interested himself in spiritual matters, the salvation of the subjects that he felt he had been called to lead. He intervened energetically in the case of the Donatist schism in North Africa, which followed the great persecutions. The Donatists had refused to recognize those Christians who had denied the Church during the persecutions. In spite of the intervention of both the emperor and the pope (Council of Arles, 314), the schism lasted for a whole century until the Church in Africa was subsequently destroyed by the Vandals. In 325 Constantine convoked the Council of Nicaea, which condemned the heresy of Arius of Alexandria who had called into doubt the divinity of Christ. In 381 the Council of Constantinople met to ensure the enactment of the decisions taken at Nicaea. Constantine played a decisive role in the build-ing of basilicas and churches in the great cities of the empire and in the holy sites in Palestine.

The fourth century saw the flourishing of a Christian culture that stressed the values of the classical heritage to which religious inspiration gave a fresh vigor. It was in this context that Emperor Julian, who succeeded Constantius II in 360, surprisingly reconverted to paganism and gave rise to a new persecution of the Christians, which ended with Julian's death in 363.

The second half of the fourth century is called 'the golden age' of the Fathers of the Church: Athanasius of Alexandria (c. 295-373), Basil of Caesarea (c. 329-370), Gregory of Nazianzus (330-390), Gregory of Nyssa (332-394), Evagrios of Pontus (345-399), John Chrysostom (c. 344/54-398/407), Theodore of Mopsuestia (c. 350-428), John Cassian (c. 365-435), Augustine

*1. Constantine, the Roman emperor who converted to Christianity. He removed the threat of persecution within the Roman empire. He also tried to closely connect Christianity with political power.*

*2. A Coptic bas relief shows two angels holding the crown of victory with a cross in the center. The crown is common in Hellenistic art, but the cross is a Christian symbol. Here, the symbol of pagan 'victories' is replaced by the cross of Christ, which defeats all evil.*
*3. A modern rebuilding of an early-Christian village on the shores of Lake Geneva, Switzerland. It was the origin of the city of Geneva. The church is hard to recognize among the houses. The church was originally used only for baptisms, while the Eucharistic sacrifice took place in an adjacent house. Eventually the celebration of the Eucharistic moved to the church.*
*4. The great church, or basilica, at Trier, Germany. It was the basis of future Christian churches, that were similar to the old Roman public assembly buildings.*
*5. A Roman building in Maktar, Tunisia that was originally a gymnasium for young men. It eventually became a Christian church.*

of Hippo (354-430), Jerome (c. 347-419), Ambrose of Milan (c. 339-397), Martin of Tours (316-397), Damasus of Rome (c. 305-384), and Hilary of Poitiers (c. 315-367). All of these were great writers and fine stylists, in addition to being important theologians who gave the Church a fundamental doctrinal base in both the East and the West. Most of them became bishops before their death. Their influence as theologians and bishops made this period crucial in Church history. They provided the groundwork of an entire religious culture organized around faith and spiritual life—a culture that embraced all aspects of life.

# THE END OF THE ANCIENT WORLD

*1.* Saint Augustine, from a painting by Simone Martini currently in Cambridge, England. Saint Augustine wrote The City of God.
*2.* The Heavenly Jerusalem from a tile mosaic in a triumphal arch of San Vitale in Ravenna in Italy.

*3.* Mexico City is one of the largest cities in the world today. It is a place where skyscrapers stand next to slums. Still, in such a place of inequality, Christian communities enjoy unity, or fraternal solidarity. They provide good news of man's spiritual destiny in the Celestial City.

3

In 410 A.D. Augustine, a polished writer and the well-known bishop of Hippo in North Africa, started writing *The City of God*, a work of twenty-two books, which would take him fifteen years of his life. This monument of the literary culture of the Late Empire is also the first philosophy of history. A great authority on his own times, Augustine understood that pagan intellectuals were not interested in the modern cults but looked nostalgically back at the grandeur of ancient Rome.

Starting at the very origins of the story of humanity, Augustine refers to Cain, the builder of the earthly city, and to Abel, who is only a pilgrim from the celestial city, and whose mission is continued by Abraham and the people of Israel. By means of intricate symbolism about the states of antiquity, Au-

gustine arrives at Rome and demonstrates the triumphal failure of the glory of conquests, of the thirst for power, of the disregard of man, and of the emptiness of idolatry and pagan cults. His prophetic vision embraces the entire horizon of human history and he stresses the presence of a principle of growth that conforms to the Creator's plan in the development of mankind; this plan is at the origin of the history of Israel and will find its fulfillment in the coming of Christ. Thus human history has a meaning which can be discovered by means of the succession of events in sacred history and the words of the prophets. This makes Augustine conclude that 'the past centuries of history would have remained like empty jars if Christ had not come to fill them.'

# Glossary

*words in* CAPITALS *are cross references*

**Aeon**   In the ancient philosophy of GNOSTICISM, the aeons were god-like beings with everlasting powers that came from the Supreme Being. The Supreme Being used the aeons to create action in the universe.

**Agape**   In Greek Christian communities, an agape was a meal for people in need of help and was given as a sign of love and goodwill. This Greek word meant 'the tenderness which comes from God.'

**Apologists**   Apologists were Greek and Latin writers who defended the Christian faith from insults and PERSECUTIONS from the PAGANS, during the second and third centuries. The apologists wrote about the spiritual beliefs of Christians, and also their feelings and engagements about the ancient world's traditions and culture.

**Apostolic tradition**   In the second century, the Christian Church opposed the philosophy of GNOSTICISM. These gnostic ideas understood Christian doctrines or beliefs quite differently. Against the wishes of the gnostic priest, MARCION, the Church decided the canon, which was the official list of books in the New Testament. The Church proved that this list contained the whole and truthful Christian faith, also known as the apostolic tradition. The Church also proved that this faith was agreed upon by the whole Church (Irenaeus of Lyon, Tertullian). The apostolic tradition forms the rule of religious faith (Clement of Alexandria).

**Arian, Arianism**   Arianism was a religious belief first preached by the priest, Arius, in 320 A.D. Arius thought that Jesus Christ, the Son, was lower to God, the Father, in rank, power, and glory. His theory was judged to be wrong by the COUNCIL of Nicaea in 325 A.D. His followers still believed him, though. It was only the Council of Constantinople in 381 A.D. that decided the matter by establishing the belief of a Trinity: a God or divine nature in three separate persons.

**Baptism**   The word baptism comes from a Latin term which means 'immersion' or dipping into water. From the earliest centuries, new believers were plunged completely in running water. This baptism was a symbol of the death and resurrection of Jesus Christ. Believers then began a new regenerated life as sons of God.

**Cemetery, coemeterium**   Cemetery is from the Greek word meaning 'place where one sleeps.' For both Jews and Christians, the word meant 'the burying of the dead.' To them, the idea of sleeping was connected to believing in the resurrection (or rebirth) of the dead as a re-awakening. Also, the word *depositio* meant 'a temporary deposition.'

**Coenobitism, Coenobite**   Coenobitism comes from the Greek word meaning 'those who live in a community.' In Egypt, following the example of Anthony (250-356 A.D.), some Christians became known as 'anchorites.' They wanted to seek a holy life in the quiet of the desert. In 320 A.D., Pachomius organized a community in Thebes and from there coenobitism spread both West and East. A similar movement, the MONASTICISM of Egypt, founded a way of life which inspired Saint Benedict when he organized his community.

**Council**   A group of bishops gathered to discuss and decide upon Church problems and questions was called a council. An 'ecumenical council' brought together bishops from the whole Church. Smaller, more local, councils were held by the Church as early as the second century A.D. The first ecumenical council was held at Nicaea in 325 A.D.

**Donatism**   Donatism was a SCHISM of the North African Christian Church as a result of the PERSECUTION of 303-305 A.D. It was thought some bishops and priests had betrayed the Church by giving holy writings to the persecutors. The argument between Donatists and Catholics was about the personality of the Church: How should the Church interact, as a group, with the world and its institutions? Donatism was gone completely by the time of the Muslim invasions.

**Elkesaism**   Elkesaism was the faith followed by some Judeo-Christian baptists who believed that they could purify themselves and be spiritually saved by two special ceremonies. The believer's body was washed with a daily BAPTISM in water. The believer's food was also made holy, purified, by water. This belief first came from Hebrew laws and became very popular. The whole Middle East practiced these ceremonies in the second and third centuries. The philosopher, Mani, lived in an Elkesaite community for twenty years.

**Encratism**   Encratism was a spiritual discipline that was not trusted by the early Church. It turned away all goods created by God, forbade eating meat, and rejected marriage. The Fathers of the Christian Church were against these teachings. They worried Encratism could be confused with another spiritual discipline, MONASTICISM, that was helpful to the Church. The Fathers also thought Encratism threatened the state of peace in the Christian world.

**Eucharist**   Eucharist is a Greek word meaning 'thanksgiving.' This ceremony of breaking bread at the table and dividing it among the guests is similar to a Jewish meal. For early Christians, this became the sign of their unity. It was a symbol of their coming together with Jesus Christ, just as he had promised during the Last Supper. The eucharist is also known as 'the breaking of the bread' and has always been the most special ceremony in Christianity.

**Gnosticism**   A philosophy that, at one time, included several different schools of philosophy and religious groups. There are three main ideas to gnosticism: The belief that man possessed an awareness, a gnosis, which gave intelligence through the work of God; An understanding of opposites such as the evil, material world opposite the bright, spiritual one; The idea of an unending emptiness, the cosmos, that was caused by a 'crisis in the divine,' a sort of trouble in heaven. This crisis made a god-like being, an AEON, fall from the universe, the PLEROMA.

**Heresy**   Heresy is either one person who wrongly believes a religious rule that is not believed by the rest of Christians, or a group who follows an error-filled version of Christianity. The heretic thinks and lives separated from the rest of the Christian community. He becomes an enemy of the faith and cuts himself off from 'the rule of life.'

**Idolatry**   Idolatry is a belief in idols and the worship of idols. The early Christians opposed all groups that worshiped false idols. It was considered to be an error and a moral sin. The controversy against idols prevented Christians who had converted from PAGANISM from returning to the temples and participating in their old religion.

**Initiation rites**   Initiation rites often take place in a religious ceremony.  They symbolize a passage from one sort of life to another, and could also be thought of as an entry or training period. Initiation includes two things: physically entering a new community, and accepting new religious values to lead a better life or to achieve a goal. Most religions use initiation rites to symbolize the entry into a holy world. The passage to the new life was, for the early Christians, first through BAPTISM and EUCHARIST. These two were considered the same, and often included calling upon the Spirit and placing oil on the forehead. Such anointing is used in the Old Testament to show a sacredness because they drew a cross on the forehead with the oil. This practice is still used by Christians during the ceremony of confirmation.

**Judaeo-Christianity**   Judaeo-Christianity is a blending of the Christian life with the Jewish life. Judaism had a strong influence on early Christianity. It gave Christianity certain biblical symbols, the belief in angels, and religious writings which tried to explain the beginning and future of mankind.

**Judaeo-Hellenism**   Judaeo-Hellenism is a blending of the Jewish life with Greek culture. This took place especially in Alexandria. Philo of Alexandria was a great supporter of this combination.

**Kerygma**   The *kerygma* is the message and proclamation of the Gospel and also of the entire early-Christian community. This message was simply, 'salvation through Jesus Christ.' The *kerygma* includes the preaching of both the Apostles and their disciples.

**Manichaeism**   Manichaeism is a type of GNOSTIC belief founded by the philosopher, Mani (216-277 A.D.). He believed that there were two basic yet different principles at the very origin of things: Light and Dark. This faith influenced all knowledge and all life. Manichaeism became an organized Church with its own Scriptures, structure of priests, traditions, and also its own missionaries called 'the elected ones.'

**Marcionism**   Marcion was a priest born in Sinope (in Pontus) who went to Rome to preach and began his own Church in 144 A.D. He thought the God of the Old Testament to be a mean and cruel god, and refused to believe God was the father of Jesus Christ. Instead, Marcion's version of God created matter and the world. Marcion rewrote the New Testament, except for Paul's letters, to suit his needs. He influenced a philosopher, Mani, who used Marcion's beliefs to develop his own GNOSTIC beliefs. This philosophy of gnosticism included two opposing yet equal forces: good and bad, light and dark.

**Monasticism**   In the second century A.D., the word *monachos* meant 'unique, loved by God in a special way.' In the fourth century A.D., some unmarried people in Egypt and Syria came together to pray. Some of them chose to live alone. Others, known as COENOBITES, lived in communities. The Church saw that these communities were living a special type of Christian life. In the East, the coenobites helped poor people, worked hard, and took on the religious duties of priests and bishops. In the West, monasticism took on more ceremonial and preaching duties.

**Mysteries**   The mysteries were cults, or secret groups of worshipers and beliefs. The name, mysteries, is from a Greek phrase that means 'keeping your mouth shut.' Some mysteries began in Greek culture, while others came from eastern Oriental cultures. The mysteries became very popular and spread first to Rome, and then to the entire Roman-Hellenistic world. The mysteries were more acceptable than Christianity to the rulers because the celebrations, representations, and ideas of the mysteries were similar to those of the official religion of the empire. The mysteries also taught men about their own spiritual future.

**Pagan, paganism**   The word *paganus* originally meant 'a countryman.' In the fourth century A.D. Christians used the word to describe a belief in false gods and its connected ceremonies, practices, and customs. The label of paganism was also used to criticize the people who shared these beliefs and took part in the ceremonies.

**Persecutions**   Persecutions were acts of violence toward Christians by their enemies. The first such acts occurred in Jerusalem, then in Rome. The persecutors had many different reasons: They wanted to stop the spread of Christianity and suspected Christians of committing secret crimes and black magic; They accused the Christians of wickedness and being against the protecting Gods of the Roman empire; They were angry that Christians wouldn't believe in the gods of Rome or in the holiness of the emperor, himself.

**Pleroma**   In the ancient philosophy of GNOSTICISM, the pleroma is the universe 'on high' full of life, harmony, and light. It is opposite the lower world full of greed, confusion, sadness, and violence. Pleroma is also the opposite of the gnostic idea of the cosmos, or an unending emptiness.

**Proselyte**   The name proselyte was given to PAGANS who had converted to Judaism. This name comes from a Greek word meaning 'stranger,' which is based on a Hebrew word, *gur*.

**Refrigerium**   This word is often found on Christian graves. It means the heavenly rest and peace, and everlasting happiness of the dead. The meaning of *refrigerium* then changed to refer to the meals held during funerals or on their anniversaries. Pagans often celebrated the anniversary of a funeral. The pagans then started to build tombs, large underground graves that were also used for funeral ceremonies.

**Remission of sins**   Remission of sins is a gift from Christ. This gift is caused by an out-pouring of his recreating and loving Spirit. Remission of sins was given to the Apostles and the people who replaced them so they could wipe away sins. It is the highest ability of a god and is mentioned in the gospels (Mt 18,18; Jn 20, 22-23).

**Sacrament**   A sacrament is an early-Christian ceremony based on a earlier Jewish ceremony. Christians and Jews disagreed that Jesus Christ was a savior who gave salvation to his followers through the good works of the Church. This idea is also conveyed through the Greek word *mysterion* and the Latin word *sacramentum*.

**Schism**   Schism is a Latin Christian word from the third century. It means a disagreement that causes one community to split into two warring groups. Schism is similar to HERESY. Heresy is a division of religious ideas within the Church, schism is a division of the people that are the Church.

**Tetrarchy**   A tetrarchy is a system of government with four people sharing control of the Roman empire. These four were known as emperors, and each controlled a different part of the Roman lands. Diocletian ruled from 284 to 305 A.D., Galerius ruled from 305 to 311 A.D., Maximian ruled from 305 to 313 A.D., and Constantius Chlorus ruled from 305 to 306 A.D.

**Vandals**   Vandals were a tribe of German people who crossed the Rhine River in 406 A.D. and invaded Gaul, Spain, and North Africa. They looted and destroyed cities in their path. By 425 A.D., the Vandals controlled Spain and followed the ARIAN faith. The Vandals began PERSECUTING people who followed the Catholic religion. In 430 A.D., they seized Hippo, the chief town in Numidia, and conquered Rome in 455 A.D. These new lands made the Vandal empire very large. Byzantine emperor Justinian conquered the Vandals in 533 A.D. The Vandals never rose to power again, but they had already destroyed Christianity in North Africa.

**Zoroastrianism** or **Mazdaism**   Zoroastrianism was the religion in the country of Iran. The Arabs then conquered Iran and the people eventually converted to the religion of the Arabs, Islam. Zoroastrianism was named after its founder, Zoroaster or Zarathustra. The alternate name, Mazdaism, comes from the religion's Supreme God, Ahura Mazda, known as the god of goodness. Mazda was the wise Lord who inspired man and led him toward goodness. Ahura Mazda fought the opposing power of Ahriman, the evil spirit.

# Index